POP'S TRUCK

Written by Honey Andersen and Bill Reinholtd
Illustrated by Pam Posey

Dan and Wendy liked going to Pop's house because he lived on a farm.

There were sheep, chickens, pigs, one cow, and an old dog to play with at Pop's farm.

But best of all, there was Pop's truck.

"Your truck is great, Pop," Dan always said.

Pop let the children ride in the back of the truck when he fed out hay to the sheep and the cow.

He let them ride in the back of the truck when he went to check the fences.

Once, he let Wendy sit in the back holding a lamb when its mother was sick.

Pop had to bring the ewe and her lamb up to the sheds, to look after them.

Dan had to sit on the ewe to keep her still, while Pop's truck bounced over the dirt road all the way home.

"Well, that's where it is," said Pop.
"I can't have useless machinery
lying around the farm.
Come and look at the new truck I bought.
It's in the garage."

"I don't even want to see it," said Wendy.
"I'd rather go to the dump
and see the old truck."

"Yes, so would I," agreed Dan.

"Well, how about a ride in the back
of the new truck, down to the dump?
You could say good-bye to the old one,"
suggested Pop.

"O.K."

Wendy and Dan ran to the garage,
and there was a very shiny, new blue truck.

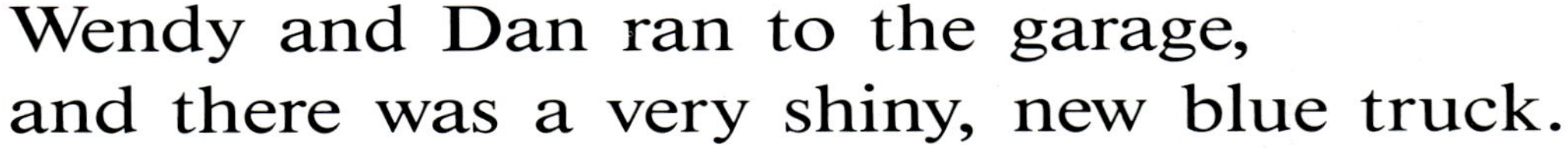

"The old truck never had to go in the garage," muttered Dan. "It was tough enough to live outside for thirty years."

"I hate blue trucks," Wendy said to Dan, as she scrambled into the back of the new truck. "And there are no old sacks in the back to sit on."

They sat quietly in the back of the truck,
while Pop drove down the driveway to the gate.
Dan hopped out, opened the gate,
and then closed it after Pop had driven through.

As they drove down the road to the dump,
they noticed that the new truck wasn't
nearly as bumpy to ride in.

“I can’t even see the old truck,”
said Wendy. “Can you, Dan?”

“No. Oh . . . Oh, yes, I mean. Look, Wendy!
There it is. It’s just over there,
by the storage shed.
But why is it up there, instead of
down in the valley with all the junk?”

The old truck was parked on the top of the hill,
with its cab and engine pointing down
into the dump. It seemed to be looking
over the whole scene.

As Pop stopped near the old truck,
the children were surprised to see that someone
was sitting in the front.

It was Dave, the man in charge of the dump.
He was having a cup of tea, and he had
his thermos propped up
on the seat next to his paper.

"Hello, Bill," he said to Pop.
"That truck of yours was just too good to bury with all the garbage.

I got the boys to haul it up here for me.
It makes a great office. It keeps me warm and dry.
It's a great old truck."

"There you are, Pop," whispered Dan.
"Why didn't you think of that?
You could have used it for an office at the farm."

"Well, Dan, you're probably right," replied Pop.
"But to tell you the truth,
I don't really need an office that badly."

"Well, at least someone can still use it," said Dan. "And it didn't have to be crushed to pieces."

"And," Wendy said to Dave, "you get a really good view from here!"

"What about coming into my office for a cup of tea?" asked Dave.

"That would be great," said Wendy.

"That would be terrific," said Dan.